INSPIRING HOCKEY STORIES FOR KIDS

Fun, Inspirational Facts & Stories For Young Readers

FALCON FOCUS

Copyright © 2023 Falcon Focus

All rights reserved. No part of this publication may be reproduced, distributed or transmitted in any form or by any means, including photocopying, recording, or other electronic or mechanical methods, without the prior written permission of the publisher, except in the case of brief quotations embodied in critical reviews and certain other non-commercial uses permitted by copyright law.

Trademarked names appear throughout this book. Rather than use a trademark symbol with every occurrence of a trademarked name, names are used in an editorial fashion, with no intention of infringement of the respective owner's trademark. The information in this book is distributed on an "as is" basis, without warranty. Although every precaution has been taken in the preparation of this work, neither the author nor the publisher shall have any liability to any person or entity with respect to any loss or damage caused or alleged to be caused directly or indirectly by the information contained in this book.

Hockey is more than a sport; it's a frozen narrative unfolding on a sheet of ice. Each glide is a chapter, every slapshot a spectacle, and every save a masterpiece crafted in the cold air. In this rink, every goal is a story of collaboration, every power play a display of skill, and every play a choreography of speed and agility. On this icy battleground, legends emerge, tenacity is proven, and every inch gained is a stride toward victory etched in the hearts of both players and fans.

Contents

Introduction	v
1. Wayne Gretzky's Early Years and Rise to Fame	1
2. The 1980 Miracle on Ice	7
3. Manon Rhéaume - Breaking Barriers	14
4. The Formation and Success of the Pittsburgh Penguins Dynasty	20
5. The Development of the National Women's Hockey League (NWHL)	27
6. The Heritage Classic - Hockey's Return to Its Roots	34
7. Jarome Iginla's Impact On and Off the Ice	40
8. The Evolution of Hockey Safety and Equipment	46
9. Bobby Orr's Revolutionary Play as a Defenseman	52
10. The Expansion of Hockey Globally	58
References	65
Bonus: Free Book!	67

Introduction

Welcome to the captivating world of *Inspiring Hockey Stories For Kids*, a collection that unveils exhilarating tales of triumph, determination, and the pure love for the game. Within these pages, you will embark on an extraordinary journey through the lives of iconic figures and significant moments that have shaped the landscape of hockey.

Each chapter unfolds a unique narrative, spotlighting iconic figures and pivotal events that have left an indelible mark on hockey's vibrant tapestry. From Wayne Gretzky's meteoric rise to Bobby Orr's revolutionary play as a defenseman, and the historic "Miracle on Ice" to the impactful stories of Manon Rhéaume and Jarome Iginla, this collection celebrates the diverse and awe-inspiring facets of the game.

Embark on a voyage through time, exploring the early struggles of the Pittsburgh Penguins, the birth of the National Women's Hockey League, and the global expansion of hockey into unexpected corners of the world. Dive deep into the Heritage Classic, an ode to the roots of hockey played under the open sky, and witness the evolution of safety standards and equipment that safeguard players in today's fast-paced game.

As we traverse continents, witness historic victories, and marvel at individual feats, you will discover not just the game's rich history but also the enduring values of teamwork, dedication, and the pursuit of excellence. These stories extend an invitation to be inspired, to dream, and to embrace the spirit of hockey—one of the world's most exhilarating and unifying sports. Let's start this journey together as we glide through the pages of history, where every goal scored and every challenge faced paints a vivid portrait of the enduring magic that is hockey.

Wayne Gretzky's Early Years and Rise to Fame

Childhood and Early Love for Hockey

Born on January 26, 1961, in Brantford, Ontario, Wayne Gretzky was introduced to hockey at an incredibly young age. His family, especially his father Walter Gretzky, played a pivotal role in nurturing his talent. Walter built a backyard rink where Wayne spent countless hours practicing, often in the frigid Canadian winters. From the age of three, Wayne's natural affinity for the game was evident. He honed his skills on the backyard rink, which Walter dubbed the "Wally Coliseum." Gretzky's early training wasn't just about physical drills; it also involved studying the game intensely. Walter taught him to read the sport, to understand where the puck was going to be, rather than where it had been. This early education laid the foundation for Gretzky's unique playing style.

Even as a young child, Gretzky's talent was unmistakable. By the age of six, he was playing in youth leagues with children several years older. Despite his small stature, his exceptional skill and understanding of the game set him apart. He regularly outplayed and outscored the older children, drawing attention from local hockey communities. His youth career is marked by extraordinary scoring feats, showcasing a level of talent rarely seen in players his age. Wayne often faced criticism and jealousy from other players and their parents due to his dominance on the ice, but he remained focused on his love for the game.

Gretzky's adolescence was marked by continued success in hockey. He quickly climbed the ranks of youth hockey leagues, shattering scoring records and gaining widespread attention. His performances in major junior hockey, particularly with the Sault Ste. Marie Greyhounds of the Ontario Hockey League (OHL), further cemented his reputation as a prodigious talent. Scouts from the National Hockey League (NHL) closely followed his career, eagerly anticipating his entry into the professional league. Wayne's time in the OHL was a critical period in his development, where he fine-tuned his skills and prepared for the challenges of professional hockey.

The early years of Wayne Gretzky's life were instrumental in shaping him into the player he would become. His family's support, relentless practice, and innate understanding of hockey set the stage for his rise to fame. This foundation, built in the small town of Brantford, Ontario, led to Gretzky becoming one of the most celebrated athletes in the history of sports, earning him the fitting nickname, "The Great One."

Record-Breaking Junior Career

Wayne Gretzky's journey through the Ontario Hockey League (OHL) is a tale of unprecedented success and early indications of a future hockey legend. Joining the OHL as a teenager, Gretzky's impact was immediate and profound. Playing for the Sault Ste. Marie Greyhounds, his talent on the ice quickly became the talk of the league. Gretzky's style, characterized by incredible anticipation and a unique ability to read the game, set him apart from his peers. His first season with the Greyhounds was a showcase of his exceptional skill and hockey intelligence. He amassed an impressive number of points, a feat even more remarkable considering his age and the level of competition in the OHL.

Gretzky's time in the OHL wasn't just about personal success; it was a period of rapid growth and development. Under the guidance of experienced coaches and surrounded by competitive peers, he refined his playing style, combining innate talent with a growing understanding of strategy and teamwork. This period was decisive in preparing Gretzky for the rigors and challenges of professional hockey. It was in the OHL that Gretzky began to develop the leadership qualities that would later define his career in the NHL. His ability to inspire and elevate the play of his teammates was evident, even at this early stage.

The records and accolades Gretzky earned during his OHL career were a precursor to his later achievements in the NHL. He broke several scoring records, some of which had stood for decades, and in doing so, he altered the expectations for what young players could achieve in junior hockey. His dominance in the OHL garnered attention from NHL scouts and team executives, who saw in Gretzky a player capable of transforming a franchise. His performances in the OHL left no doubt that he was ready for the next step in his career.

The culmination of Gretzky's time in the OHL was marked by widespread recognition of his potential to become one of the greatest hockey players of all time. He left the league not only with impressive statistics but also with a growing fan base and media attention. His transition from junior hockey to the professional ranks was eagerly anticipated by hockey enthusiasts and experts who recognized that Gretzky's blend of skill, intelligence, and dedication was something special. His OHL career set the stage for what would become a legendary journey in the NHL, paving the way for his ascent to hockey immortality.

NHL Debut and Rapid Ascent

Wayne Gretzky's entry into the National Hockey League (NHL) marked the beginning of a new era in professional hockey. His debut with the Edmonton Oilers in 1979 was highly anticipated, not just by fans in Edmonton but by the entire hockey world. Gretzky joined the NHL under unique circumstances; he was signed by the Indianapolis Racers of the World Hockey Association (WHA) and played briefly there before being sold to the Oilers, who then joined the NHL as part of the WHA-NHL merger. From his very first season, Gretzky's impact on the team and the league was profound.

In his rookie season, Gretzky tied for the league lead in scoring, an unprecedented achievement for an 18-year-old. His remarkable vision, hockey sense, and scoring ability were on full display, captivating fans and baffling opponents. Despite his young age, he quickly became the focal point of the Oilers' offense, showcasing a level of skill and maturity that belied his years. Gretzky's presence transformed the Oilers into a formidable team, setting the stage for a dynasty in the making.

Gretzky's early years in the NHL were not without challenges. His slight build and unique playing style initially led some critics to doubt his ability to endure the physicality of the NHL. However, Gretzky's intelligence on the ice, his ability to anticipate plays, and his extraordinary puck-handling skills allowed him to navigate these challenges successfully. He revolutionized the way the game was played, using his agility and mental acuity to create scoring opportunities and redefine what was possible in hockey.

The rapid ascent of Wayne Gretzky in the NHL is a story of a young man exceeding every expectation set before him. By his second season, he had won the Hart Memorial Trophy as the league's Most Valuable Player, an honor he would claim for eight consecutive years. His scoring feats, including setting the single-season points record, were not just breaking existing records; they were shattering the perceived limits of the sport. Gretzky's early years with the Edmonton Oilers laid the groundwork for what would become one of the most illustrious careers in all of sports, earning him the nickname "The Great One." His impact extended beyond the ice, as he played a key role in popularizing hockey across North America and inspiring a new generation of players and fans.

Shattering Records and Redefining the Game

Wayne Gretzky's NHL career is synonymous with record-breaking achievements and redefining the standards of hockey excellence. Throughout his illustrious career, Gretzky set numerous records, many of which still stand unchallenged, underscoring his dominance in the sport. His ability to consistently perform at an elite level, game after game, season after season, was nothing short of extraordinary.

One of the most remarkable aspects of Gretzky's career was his scoring prowess. He shattered the NHL record for most points in a single season, amassing an astounding 215 points during the 1985-86 season. This achievement was one of many instances where Gretzky not only broke a record but did so by a wide margin, creating new benchmarks that seemed almost unattainable. His scoring records include reaching 1,000 career points in the fewest games and being the only player to score over 200 points in a season, a feat he accomplished four times.

Gretzky's impact on the game extended beyond individual accolades. He led the Edmonton Oilers to four Stanley Cup victories in 1984, 1985, 1987, and 1988, cementing the team's legacy as one of the NHL's great dynasties. His leadership, combined with his exceptional play, was instrumental in these championship runs. Gretzky's presence on the ice elevated the performance of his teammates, and his vision and playmaking ability made the Oilers one of the most formidable teams in hockey history.

Gretzky's career is marked by numerous awards and honors, including winning the Hart Memorial Trophy as the league's Most Valuable Player an unprecedented nine times, the Art Ross Trophy for scoring ten times, and the Conn Smythe Trophy for the most valuable player during the playoffs twice. Beyond the hardware, Gretzky's influence changed the way hockey was played. He revolutionized the sport with his creativity, intelligence, and skill, setting a new standard for future generations.

Wayne Gretzky's legacy transcends the records and trophies. He transformed hockey into a more dynamic, exciting, and offensive game. His name became synonymous with excellence in sports, and his impact on hockey is immeasurable. Gretzky retired from the NHL in 1999, holding 61 NHL records, a testament to his unparalleled career. His number 99 was retired league-wide, an honor befitting a player who was not just a great hockey player but "The Great One." His contributions to the game, both on and off the ice, continue to inspire and influence players and fans alike, solidifying his status as one of the most extraordinary athletes in the history of sports.

The 1980 Miracle on Ice

The Backdrop of the Cold War

The 1980 Winter Olympics in Lake Placid, New York, provided the stage for one of the most remarkable moments in sports history, set against the tense backdrop of the Cold War. This period in history was marked by a geopolitical struggle between the United States and the Soviet Union, extending into various arenas, including sports. The hockey game between the USA and the USSR was more than just a contest on ice; it was a symbolic battle between two superpowers with opposing ideologies. The Soviet Union, at the time, was a powerhouse in international hockey, having won the gold medal in five of the six previous Winter Olympics. Their team consisted of seasoned, world-class athletes who were technically soldiers but played hockey full-time. In contrast, the American team was composed of amateur players, mostly college students, who had no significant experience in international play.

The political tension of the era added immense significance to the matchup. The Soviet Union's invasion of Afghanistan in 1979 heightened global tensions, leading to the USA boycotting the Summer Olympics in Moscow later that year. The game took on dimensions beyond sport, symbolizing the broader global struggle between communism and democracy. The American public, amidst this tense atmosphere, looked to their young, underdog team not just for sporting success but as a beacon of national pride and resilience.

In this context, the game was not merely viewed as a competition but as a metaphor for the struggle between the two nations. The US team, led by coach Herb Brooks, faced not only the pressure of the game but also the weight of their nation's expectations in this larger-than-life confrontation. The game was broadcast on national television, and millions of Americans tuned in, hoping for a miracle against the seemingly invincible Soviet team. The anticipation and excitement surrounding this game were unprecedented, with the political implications elevating it to a level of importance that far surpassed the boundaries of the rink.

The stage was set for what would become an iconic moment in Olympic and hockey history. The 1980 Miracle on Ice was not just a game; it was a reflection of the times, a moment when a hockey match encapsulated the hopes, fears, and tensions of an era. The underdog story of the American team, facing off against the Goliath of hockey, the Soviet Union, was a narrative that captured the imagination of a nation and became a defining symbol of the Cold War sporting rivalry. This game would go on to symbolize one of the most dramatic upsets in sports history, a tribute to the unpredictability of hockey and the enduring spirit of competition in the face of overwhelming odds.

Formation of the US Team

The formation of the 1980 US Olympic hockey team was a journey marked by unconventional choices and rigorous training, all masterminded by coach Herb Brooks. Brooks, a former Olympic player and successful college coach, was known for his innovative coaching style and deep understanding of the game. His selection process for the Olympic team was not solely based on individual talent; instead, he focused on finding players who could adapt to his unique style of play, which emphasized speed, stamina, and teamwork over traditional power play. This approach was revolutionary at the time and set the US team apart from the more traditional, physically dominant style of the Soviets.

Brooks scoured the country, attending numerous college games to identify potential candidates. He looked for players who exhibited not just skill, but also the mental toughness and adaptability he believed necessary for success on the international stage. The team he assembled was young, with an average age of just 22, making it one of the youngest in US hockey history. Many of the players were from rival colleges and had to overcome existing animosities to work as a unit. This dynamic was a crucial element of Brooks' strategy, as he believed that a team forged through shared adversity would be stronger.

The training regimen set by Brooks was grueling. He subjected the team to intense physical and mental conditioning, pushing them to their limits to build endurance and resilience. The players underwent months of exhaustive training, both on and off the ice, which included playing a series of exhibition games against teams from Europe and the US. Brooks' methods were often unorthodox and demanding, but they were designed to prepare the team not just for the physical challenge of the games, but also for the psychological warfare they would face against seasoned teams like the Soviets.

Brooks' emphasis on psychological preparation was a key component of his coaching. He sought to instill in his players a belief in their ability to compete against the world's best. His motivational tactics, which included intense, often provocative speeches and a demanding, sometimes abrasive coaching style, were aimed at building a cohesive and mentally tough team. This psychological conditioning was as crucial as physical training, as it prepared the team to handle the immense pressure and high stakes they would face in Lake Placid.

The formation of the 1980 US Olympic hockey team under Herb Brooks was a demonstration of the power of strategic planning, rigorous training, and psychological preparation. The team, comprised of young, relatively inexperienced players, was transformed into a unified, resilient unit, ready to take on the formidable challenge of competing against the world's best in a politically charged Olympic Games. Brooks' unconventional methods and his ability to inspire and unify his team were instrumental in preparing them for what would become one of the most legendary moments in sports history.

The Olympic Journey

The 1980 US Olympic hockey team's journey through the Winter Olympics in Lake Placid was a gripping tale of underdog triumph, marked by a series of unexpected victories that captured the imagination of a nation. Entering the Olympics, the US team was not considered a medal contender, especially given the presence of powerhouses like the Soviet Union and Czechoslovakia. The Soviet team, in particular, was widely regarded as the best in the world, having won the gold medal in four of the previous five Winter Olympics. The US team's underdog status was further cemented by their youth and inexperience at the international level, in stark contrast to the seasoned veterans they would face.

The US team's Olympic campaign began with a series of group-stage games, where they would need to perform well to advance to the medal round. Their first game, against Sweden, set the tone for their Olympic run. Trailing late in the game, the US team managed a dramatic last-minute goal to tie the game, demonstrating their resilience and tenacity. This result was followed by a string of victories against teams like Czechoslovakia, Norway, Romania, and West Germany. Each win bolstered the team's confidence and belief in their ability to compete at the highest level.

The victory against Czechoslovakia was particularly significant. The Czechoslovak team was considered one of the best in the tournament, and a strong showing against them was crucial for the US team's chances of advancing. The US team's decisive 7-3 win was a shock to many and served as a statement that they were a force to be reckoned with. This game was a turning point, altering the perception of the US team both within the Olympic Village and back home in the United States.

As the US team advanced to the medal round, their underdog story captured the hearts and minds of the American public. The Cold War undercurrents added a layer of geopolitical drama to the sporting event, turning their games into must-watch TV for millions. Each victory was celebrated as a symbol of American grit and determination, resonating far beyond the realm of sports. The team's unity, work ethic, and unyielding spirit were reflective of the values that resonated with the American audience.

The culmination of their Olympic journey was the seminal game against the Soviet Union, known as the "Miracle on Ice." But the story didn't end there. After defeating the Soviets, the US team still had to win one more game to secure the gold medal. Their final match against Finland was another display of the team's resilience. Trailing after two periods, the US team mounted a comeback in the third period, securing a victory and clinching the gold medal.

The 1980 US Olympic hockey team's journey was a remarkable saga of overcoming odds, defying expectations, and achieving the seemingly impossible. Their path through the Winter Olympics was not just a series of hockey games; it was a narrative of perseverance, unity, and the triumph of the underdog. This team, once considered a long shot, etched their names into the annals of sports history, leaving a legacy that continues to inspire.

The Historic Victory

The game against the Soviet Union on February 22, 1980, stands as one of the most iconic moments in Olympic history, often referred to as the "Miracle on Ice." The Soviet team, composed of seasoned veterans, was heavily favored to win. They had dominated international hockey for years and were considered virtually unbeatable. In contrast, the US team, comprised of college athletes and amateur players, was the clear underdog. The game, therefore, was not just a sporting contest but a David versus Goliath matchup that resonated with symbolic significance during the Cold War era.

Coach Herb Brooks' strategy for the US team was rooted in a fast-paced, aggressive style of play, designed to counter the Soviet team's skill and experience. Brooks knew that matching the Soviets in their traditional style of play was not feasible. Instead, he focused on a strategy that leveraged his team's strengths: youth, speed, and endurance. He instilled a belief in his players that they could compete with and beat the Soviet team by playing a relentless, high-energy game.

The game began with the Soviet Union taking an early lead, which was not unexpected given their prowess. However, the US team did not falter under the pressure. They responded with resilience, tying the game, and then taking the lead in the third period. The Americans' performance was characterized by relentless forechecking, disciplined defense, and opportunistic scoring. Goalie Jim Craig's exceptional performance was crucial, as he made several key saves, keeping the US team in the game against the relentless Soviet attack.

As the final seconds of the game ticked down and the US team maintained their lead, the realization of what they were about to achieve began to sink in. The final buzzer marked not just a victory in a hockey game, but an upset for the ages. The US team's win was a seismic event in the sports world, sending shockwaves beyond the ice rink. It was a victory that transcended sports, symbolizing hope and resilience during a time of geopolitical tension.

The impact of this victory on the sport of hockey and the nation was profound. It popularized hockey in the United States, inspiring a generation of players and fans. The game was a defining moment in Olympic history, a testament to the spirit of competition and the unpredictability of sports. For the American public, the victory was a source of immense national pride, a bright spot during a time of economic and political challenges. The "Miracle on Ice" became a symbol of what could be achieved against overwhelming odds, a story of underdogs triumphing against the giants. This historic victory remains etched in the collective memory of the nation, a sporting achievement that continues to inspire and resonate with the story of the ultimate underdog victory.

Manon Rhéaume - Breaking Barriers

Early Life and Introduction to Hockey

Manon Rhéaume's journey in hockey, marked by groundbreaking achievements and barrier-breaking moments, began in the small town of Beauport, Quebec. Born on February 24, 1972, Rhéaume was introduced to hockey at a young age, a path influenced significantly by her family's passion for the sport. Her father, a coach, played a pivotal role in nurturing her interest in hockey. Growing up in a hockey-loving household, Rhéaume quickly developed a love for the game, often playing with her brothers and neighborhood kids. From the outset, it was clear that she had a natural talent and a deep passion for the sport. Unlike many girls her age, Rhéaume did not gravitate towards figure skating or other sports typically associated with girls; her heart was firmly set on hockey.

Rhéaume's early experiences on the ice were not in girls' leagues, as opportunities for girls in hockey were extremely limited at the time. Instead, she played on boys' teams, competing against and alongside male players. This was a challenging path, fraught with obstacles both on and off the ice. She often faced skepticism and criticism for playing a sport that was predominantly male-dominated. However, Rhéaume's determination and skill quickly silenced doubters as she proved herself to be not just a capable player, but a standout, even among her male peers. Her time playing with boys' teams was not merely about competing; it was about breaking down gender barriers in a sport that had very few female role models.

Rhéaume's talent as a goaltender became increasingly evident as she progressed through youth hockey. Her agility, reflexes, and understanding of the game set her apart. Playing in goal, a position that requires a unique blend of mental and physical skills, Rhéaume demonstrated remarkable prowess. She developed a reputation as a tough, resilient goaltender, capable of holding her own against powerful shots and aggressive plays. Her success in these early years laid the groundwork for her historic achievements to come.

These formative years in Quebec were instrumental in shaping Rhéaume's future in hockey. They were years marked by persistence, resilience, and a pioneering spirit. Manon Rhéaume's early experiences in the world of boys' and men's hockey paved the way for her future success and her role as a trailblazer in the sport. Her journey from the rinks of Beauport to breaking barriers on the international stage is a testament to her skill, determination, and the courage it took to challenge the norms of the hockey world.

Making History in the NHL

Manon Rhéaume's exhibition game appearance with the Tampa Bay Lightning on September 23, 1992, was a historic event that broke the gender barrier in the National Hockey League (NHL). Her stepping onto the ice to face the St. Louis Blues in a preseason game was unprecedented, making her the first and only woman to play in the NHL. This moment transcended the sport of hockey, becoming a significant milestone in the history of women in professional sports. Rhéaume, a goaltender, was no stranger to breaking barriers in a male-dominated sport, but playing in the NHL was a feat that many thought impossible for a woman. Her appearance with the Lightning was not merely a symbolic gesture; it was a testament to her skill and dedication to the game of hockey.

During the game, Rhéaume faced shots from professional NHL players, showcasing her talent at the highest level of the sport. While she allowed two goals, her performance was noteworthy for its poise and resilience under the intense pressure and scrutiny of the moment. Rhéaume's participation in the game challenged long-standing perceptions about the role and capabilities of women in sports, especially in leagues traditionally dominated by men. Her presence on the ice opened the door for conversations about women's participation in professional sports and served as an inspiration to countless young female athletes who aspired to compete at the highest levels.

The impact of Rhéaume's appearance in an NHL game was far-reaching, extending beyond the boundaries of the hockey rink. It was a pivotal moment in the ongoing struggle for gender equality in sports and highlighted the need for greater opportunities and recognition for female athletes. Rhéaume's courage and perseverance in breaking through a significant gender barrier paved the way for future generations of athletes, proving that with talent and determination, gender should not be a limiting factor in reaching the pinnacle of any sport. Her historic game with the Tampa Bay Lightning remains a landmark achievement in sports history, symbolizing the breaking of glass ceilings and challenging the status quo in professional athletics.

Impact on Women's Hockey

Manon Rhéaume's influence on women's hockey extends far beyond her historic appearance in the NHL. Her role in the development and promotion of the sport for women has been pivotal, making significant contributions both on and off the ice. Rhéaume's participation in women's hockey at the international level, particularly in the Women's World Championships and the Olympics, showcased her exceptional talent and helped elevate the profile of women's hockey on the global stage. As a goaltender for the Canadian national team, Rhéaume played a critical role in the team's successes. Her performances in the Women's World Championships were especially noteworthy. Competing against the best female hockey players in the world, Rhéaume's skill and competitiveness were on full display. She helped lead Canada to gold medals, demonstrating not only her abilities but also the high level of play in women's hockey.

Her participation in the 1998 Winter Olympics in Nagano, Japan, was another significant milestone. The 1998 Olympics were the first to feature women's ice hockey as a medal sport, marking a significant moment in the history of the Olympics and women's sports. Rhéaume was an integral part of the Canadian national team, contributing to their silver medal win. This achievement was not just about the medal; it represented the growing recognition and respect for women's hockey internationally. Rhéaume's Olympic experience brought her talents to a wider audience, further inspiring young girls and women to pursue hockey.

Beyond her achievements in international competitions, Rhéaume has been a prominent advocate for women's hockey. Her groundbreaking career has inspired countless young girls to lace up skates and take to the ice, many of whom might not have considered playing hockey before seeing Rhéaume in the net. She has been a role model and a trailblazer, demonstrating that women can compete at the highest levels of the sport. Her involvement in various initiatives and programs aimed at promoting women's hockey has helped to increase participation and interest in the sport, contributing to its growth and development at the grassroots level.

Manon Rhéaume's impact on women's hockey is immeasurable. Her accomplishments as a player, combined with her advocacy and promotional efforts, have significantly advanced the sport. She has not only broken barriers and set records but has also played a key role in changing perceptions and increasing opportunities for women in hockey. Rhéaume's legacy in women's hockey is enduring, and her influence will continue to be felt for generations to come, as she has paved the way for future female hockey players to dream big and achieve greatness in the sport.

Legacy and Advocacy

Manon Rhéaume's legacy in the world of hockey is characterized by her pioneering spirit and relentless advocacy for women's participation in the sport. Beyond her remarkable achievements on the ice, Rhéaume has been a vocal and influential advocate for gender equality in hockey, tirelessly working to create more opportunities for women in the sport at all levels. Her journey from a young girl playing on boys' teams in Quebec to making history in the NHL and competing internationally has inspired a generation of female athletes to pursue their dreams in a sport once dominated by men.

Rhéaume's role in breaking down barriers has extended well beyond her playing career. She has been actively involved in initiatives and programs aimed at empowering young girls and women in hockey. Her efforts have not only increased the visibility of women's hockey but have also contributed to a greater acceptance and respect for female athletes in the sport. Through public speaking, coaching, and mentoring, Rhéaume has used her platform to advocate for equality and to encourage young girls to play hockey.

Her advocacy has had a tangible impact on the growth of women's hockey. Participation numbers have seen a significant rise, and the quality of play at the women's international level has improved dramatically, in part due to the pathways and inspiration Rhéaume helped create. She has been instrumental in showing that women's hockey is not just a novelty but a competitive and exciting sport in its own right. The advancements in women's professional hockey leagues and the increasing number of scholarships and development programs for female hockey players can be attributed, in part, to the groundwork laid by Rhéaume and her advocacy.

Manon Rhéaume's influence extends beyond tangible achievements and accolades; it lies in the hope and possibility she represents for future generations. Her story is one of breaking the mold and challenging the status quo, making her an enduring symbol of progress in the fight for gender equality in sports. Rhéaume's legacy is not just about what she accomplished as a goaltender but about the doors she opened for others. She has paved the way for young girls to dream of playing hockey at the highest levels, and her advocacy ensures that these dreams are increasingly within reach. Rhéaume's dedication to promoting women's hockey continues to inspire and empower, making her legacy a lasting and impactful one in the world of sports.

The Formation and Success of the Pittsburgh Penguins Dynasty

Team's Early History

The Pittsburgh Penguins' journey in the National Hockey League (NHL) began in 1967 when the team was established as part of the league's expansion. Named after the bird featured in their arena, the Pittsburgh Civic Arena, popularly known as "The Igloo," the Penguins embarked on what would become a storied history in professional hockey. The early years of the franchise were characterized by growing pains and challenges typical of an expansion team in a competitive league. The Penguins struggled to find their footing in the early seasons, grappling with the difficulties of building a competitive roster and establishing a fan base in a city with a rich sports culture.

In these formative years, the Penguins experienced a series of highs and lows, as is often the case with new franchises. They faced the challenge of competing against well-established teams with strong rosters, which often meant enduring losing streaks and seasons without playoff appearances. Despite these struggles, the team showed glimpses of potential and promise. The Penguins worked diligently to acquire talented players through drafts and trades, laying the groundwork for future success. Key early players who contributed to the team's development included Les Binkley, the first starting goaltender, and Andy Bathgate, a seasoned veteran who brought leadership and experience.

The Penguins' journey through the 1970s and early 1980s was a rollercoaster of successes and setbacks. While they had periods of strong performance and playoff appearances, consistency was a challenge. Financial difficulties also plagued the team, leading to uncertainty about the franchise's future. However, these challenges did not deter the organization's determination to build a winning team. The Penguins' perseverance through these early struggles set the stage for the remarkable success that would follow. The foundation laid in these initial years, through the development of a loyal fan base and the acquisition of key players, was crucial for the dynasty that the Penguins would eventually become. The early history of the Pittsburgh Penguins is a story of resilience and determination, a narrative that would define the franchise's character and contribute to its eventual rise to the top of the hockey world.

Arrival of Mario Lemieux

The Pittsburgh Penguins' trajectory took a dramatic turn with the arrival of Mario Lemieux, who was drafted first overall in 1984. This pivotal moment marked the beginning of a new era for the franchise. Lemieux, a phenomenally talented center from Montreal, brought a spark of hope to a team that had been struggling for years to make a significant impact in the NHL.

From his very first game, Lemieux's extraordinary skill was evident. He scored a goal on his first shift, signaling the start of what would be one of the most illustrious careers in hockey history. His presence on the team transformed the Penguins' fortunes and brought a new level of excitement and expectation to the fan base.

Lemieux's impact on the Penguins was immediate and profound. His exceptional ability to control the game, combined with his scoring prowess, made him one of the most dominant players in the league. He was not just a goal-scorer; he was a playmaker who elevated the performance of everyone around him. His size, skill, and hockey intelligence made him nearly unstoppable on the ice. Lemieux's presence turned the Penguins into playoff contenders and rejuvenated the team's fan base. His contributions extended beyond the ice; he became the face of the franchise, bringing attention and prestige to the team.

Throughout his career, Lemieux faced significant challenges, including serious health issues and injuries. Despite these obstacles, he consistently demonstrated resilience and a remarkable ability to return to the game at a high level. His comebacks from adversity were as impressive as his on-ice achievements, further solidifying his status as one of the game's greats.

Lemieux's influence on the Penguins was transformative. Under his leadership, the team won their first Stanley Cup in 1991, a victory that marked the culmination of years of effort and the realization of the potential that Lemieux brought to the team. This triumph was followed by another Stanley Cup win in 1992, cementing the Penguins' status as a powerhouse in the NHL.

Mario Lemieux's journey with the Pittsburgh Penguins is a story of talent, perseverance, and transformation. He not only lifted the Penguins to new heights but also left an indelible mark on the sport. His legacy with the team is defined by his incredible achievements, his role in bringing success to the franchise, and his enduring influence on the game of hockey. Lemieux's career is a testament to the impact a single player can have on a team's destiny, solidifying his place as one of the greatest players in the history of the sport.

The Crosby Era and Continued Success

The drafting of Sidney Crosby in 2005 marked the beginning of a new chapter in the Pittsburgh Penguins' history, heralding an era of continued success and dominance in the NHL. Crosby, often referred to as "Sid the Kid" in his early years, was selected first overall in the 2005 NHL Entry Draft. His arrival came at a crucial time for the Penguins, who were rebuilding after several challenging seasons. Crosby, with his exceptional talent and leadership qualities, quickly became the cornerstone of the franchise. From the outset, Crosby demonstrated why he was one of the most highly touted prospects in hockey history. His rookie season was spectacular, as he finished with an impressive 102 points, instantly proving his ability to perform at the highest level of the sport. His skill, vision, and hockey intelligence set him apart, and he soon became one of the most influential players in the league.

Crosby's impact on the Penguins was transformative. He brought a renewed sense of hope and excitement to the team and its fans. His ability to elevate the play of his teammates, combined with his own scoring and playmaking prowess, turned the Penguins into a formidable force in the NHL. Under Crosby's leadership, the team consistently performed at a high level, making deep runs in the playoffs and re-establishing themselves as a top team in the league. Crosby's role in leading the team to multiple Stanley Cup victories cannot be overstated. The Penguins won the Stanley Cup in 2009, 2016, and 2017, with Crosby playing a pivotal role in each of these triumphs. His performances in critical games, especially in the playoffs, were a showcase of his skill, determination, and clutch play. Crosby's ability to perform under pressure and his knack for scoring key goals at crucial moments were instrumental in these championship runs.

Sidney Crosby's rise to stardom was marked not just by his individual achievements but also by his ability to make those around him better. He developed into a true leader, both on and off the ice, embodying the qualities of a captain who leads by example. His work ethic, dedication to the sport, and commitment to excellence set a standard for the entire team. Crosby's influence extended beyond scoring points; he played a significant role in fostering a winning culture within the Penguins organization. His presence provided stability and a vision for the future, ensuring the team remained competitive year after year.

Sidney Crosby's era with the Pittsburgh Penguins is characterized by remarkable achievements and a legacy of success. His contribution to the team's multiple Stanley Cup victories and his consistent high-level performance have solidified his status as one of the greatest players of his generation. Crosby's impact on the Penguins is profound, not only in terms of the trophies and accolades but also in how he has helped to maintain the team's status as a powerhouse in the NHL. His journey with the Penguins is a testament to his extraordinary talent and leadership, and his influence on the team and the sport of hockey will be felt for many years to come.

Cultural and Community Impact

The Pittsburgh Penguins' influence extends far beyond the confines of the ice rink, deeply impacting the cultural and community fabric of Pittsburgh. The team's success, particularly during the eras of Mario Lemieux and Sidney Crosby, has played a significant role in shaping the city's identity and spirit. In Pittsburgh, a city renowned for its passionate sports fans and rich sports history, the Penguins have created a unique and fervent fanbase. The team's achievements, especially their multiple Stanley Cup victories, have instilled a sense of pride and unity among the residents. This connection between the team and the city is evident in the widespread support and enthusiasm displayed by fans, whether through packed games at the PPG Paints Arena or the sea of black and gold in local communities.

The Penguins' impact on Pittsburgh goes beyond just generating city pride and enthusiasm for hockey. The team has been actively involved in various community initiatives and charitable efforts, strengthening their bond with the city and its residents. Through community outreach programs, youth hockey initiatives, and partnerships with local charities, the Penguins have contributed to the betterment of the Pittsburgh community. These efforts have not only endeared the team to the residents but have also played a role in addressing important social and community issues.

Moreover, the Penguins' success and popularity have been instrumental in popularizing hockey across new regions, particularly in the United States. The team's exciting style of play, led by charismatic stars like Lemieux and Crosby, has attracted new fans to the sport, many of whom were previously unfamiliar with hockey. The Penguins have been at the forefront of growing the game of hockey, both locally and nationally. Their captivating playoff runs and engaging community programs have introduced the sport to a broader audience, contributing to the increasing popularity of hockey in regions where it was not traditionally followed.

The cultural and community impact of the Pittsburgh Penguins is a reflection of the powerful role sports teams can play in a city's identity and social fabric. They have not just been a successful hockey team; they have been a unifying force in Pittsburgh, bringing people together and contributing positively to the community. Their influence has extended beyond the arena, leaving a lasting imprint on the city and its people. The Penguins' role in popularizing hockey, their community engagement, and the deep connection they have forged with their fanbase are key aspects of their legacy, making them an integral part of Pittsburgh's cultural and social landscape.

The Development of the National Women's Hockey League (NWHL)

Founding of the NWHL

The National Women's Hockey League (NWHL) was established in 2015, marking a significant milestone in the history of women's sports. It became the first professional women's hockey league in North America to pay its players, heralding a new era of opportunity and recognition for female hockey athletes. The league's formation was a response to the growing demand for a professional platform for women's hockey, a space where female players could showcase their talent and passion for the game at a competitive level. The NWHL's inception was a culmination of years of advocacy, dedication, and hard work by numerous individuals committed to advancing women's hockey.

The league's foundation was driven by the vision of creating a sustainable professional environment for women's hockey. Dani

Rylan, the founder and first commissioner of the NWHL, played a pivotal role in turning this vision into a reality. The goal was to provide female hockey players with opportunities similar to those available to their male counterparts in the NHL. This included not just the chance to play professionally but also to be compensated for their skill and dedication to the sport. The NWHL began with four teams: the Boston Pride, Buffalo Beauts, Connecticut Whale, and New York Riveters (later renamed the Metropolitan Riveters). Each team was located in a market with a strong hockey presence, aiming to tap into the existing fan base and generate local support.

The launch of the NWHL was a significant step forward in promoting women's hockey. It provided a much-needed platform for top female players to continue their careers beyond college or international competition. The league opened doors for players to pursue hockey at a professional level, offering a space to display their talents and inspire the next generation of female hockey players. This development was crucial not only for the players but also for the growth of the sport, as it provided young girls with role models and a clear pathway to pursue hockey professionally.

The establishment of the NWHL was met with enthusiasm and support from the hockey community, including fans, players, and sponsors. It represented a major stride in the journey towards equality in sports, challenging the status quo and redefining the landscape of professional hockey. The league's formation was a bold statement about the value and potential of women's hockey, and it set the stage for continued growth and development of the sport. The NWHL's founding has had a lasting impact, contributing significantly to the visibility and viability of women's hockey as a professional sport.

Challenges Faced

The early years of the National Women's Hockey League (NWHL) were fraught with a variety of challenges, ranging from financial constraints to logistical hurdles and societal barriers. As a pioneering venture in professional women's hockey, the NWHL had to navigate a landscape that was largely uncharted and, at times, unwelcoming. One of the most pressing challenges was financial sustainability. Securing adequate funding and sponsorship was a constant battle. Unlike well-established men's leagues, the NWHL did not have a significant influx of revenue from television deals or high-profile sponsors at its inception. The league had to be creative in its approach to generating income, relying heavily on ticket sales, merchandise, and smaller-scale sponsorships. This financial uncertainty impacted various aspects of the league, including player salaries, team operations, and overall growth.

Logistical challenges were also a significant hurdle. Organizing a new professional sports league involves a complex array of tasks, from scheduling games to ensuring suitable venues and managing travel arrangements. The NWHL had to coordinate these logistics while working within the constraints of a limited budget, which often meant finding cost-effective solutions without compromising the quality of the players' experience. Balancing these logistical demands while striving to maintain a high standard of professionalism was a continual challenge for the league's management.

Additionally, the NWHL faced societal challenges, particularly in terms of visibility and support. Women's sports historically have received less media coverage and public attention compared to men's sports. The NWHL had to work tirelessly to gain media exposure and build a fan base. This effort involved not just marketing and promotion but also battling entrenched societal perceptions about women's sports. The league had to convince potential fans, sponsors, and media outlets that women's hockey was worth watching and supporting.

Despite these obstacles, the NWHL persisted, driven by a commitment to growing women's hockey and providing professional opportunities for female athletes. The league's early years were a testament to resilience and determination in the face of significant challenges. The NWHL's efforts to overcome financial, logistical, and societal barriers laid a foundation for the future growth and success of the league. These challenges, while daunting, also served as catalysts for innovation and progress, pushing the league to find creative solutions and forge new paths in the world of professional women's hockey.

Significant Milestones

Throughout its history, the National Women's Hockey League (NWHL) has achieved several significant milestones that have contributed to its growth and prominence in the world of professional sports. These milestones are not just markers of progress but also reflections of the league's dedication to advancing women's hockey. One of the key milestones in the NWHL's history was the signing of its first major sponsorship deal. This sponsorship was a crucial step in establishing the league's credibility and financial stability. It signaled to the broader sports community that women's hockey was a viable and valuable market. The backing of a major sponsor provided the league with much-needed resources and helped to increase its visibility.

Another notable milestone was the NWHL's first nationally televised game. This broadcast was a significant achievement in terms of media exposure and represented a breakthrough in bringing women's hockey to a wider audience. The televised game not only showcased the high level of competition in the league but also brought the excitement and talent of NWHL players into the homes of sports fans across the country. This increased exposure was instrumental in attracting new fans and sponsors to the league.

The NWHL has also formed several important partnerships throughout its history. These partnerships, with various organizations and entities, have been vital in expanding the league's reach and impact. From collaborations with youth hockey programs to partnerships with equipment manufacturers and other professional sports teams, these alliances have provided the NWHL with additional resources and opportunities to promote the league and its players.

Additionally, the NWHL has reached milestones in terms of expansion. The addition of new teams to the league has been a key factor in its growth. Expanding the league's footprint has not only increased the level of competition but also brought professional women's hockey to new markets. This expansion has been fundamental in building a broader fan base and providing more opportunities for female hockey players to compete at a professional level.

These milestones represent more than just achievements in the league's timeline; they are indicative of the NWHL's ongoing efforts to promote and elevate women's hockey. Each milestone has played a part in shaping the league and has contributed to its mission of providing a platform for female athletes to showcase their talents and passion for the sport. The NWHL's history is marked by these significant moments, each a step forward in the league's journey toward greater recognition and success.

Impact on Women's Hockey

The National Women's Hockey League (NWHL) has had a profound impact on the advancement of women's hockey, influencing various aspects of the sport from the grassroots to the professional level. The creation of the NWHL marked a significant step in providing female athletes with professional opportunities in hockey, a sport where such opportunities were previously limited. By establishing a professional league for women, the NWHL has not only given elite female hockey players a platform to continue their careers after college or international play but has also set a new standard for the sport. The presence of a professional league has been crucial in legitimizing women's hockey as a career path, encouraging more women to pursue the sport at a high level.

The NWHL's influence extends to youth participation in hockey. The league's players serve as role models for young girls who aspire to play hockey, demonstrating that there is a future in the sport beyond amateur levels. The visibility of female hockey players in a professional setting has inspired a new generation of young girls to lace up skates and hit the ice. The NWHL has actively engaged in community outreach and youth development programs, further fostering interest and participation in women's hockey. These initiatives not only promote the sport but also empower young girls, showing them the possibilities within hockey.

Internationally, the NWHL has played a role in increasing the visibility of women's hockey. By providing a platform for top female hockey players from around the world to showcase their skills, the league has contributed to the global recognition of the sport. The presence of international players in the NWHL has also facilitated cross-cultural exchange and learning, enriching the experience for both players and fans. This international aspect has helped to raise the standard of play and competitiveness in the league, contributing to the overall growth of women's hockey worldwide.

Moreover, the NWHL has been instrumental in advocating for better conditions and more opportunities for female athletes in hockey. From pushing for fair pay to ensuring better facilities and resources, the league's efforts have highlighted the need for equality in sports. The NWHL's existence challenges the status quo and pushes the boundaries of what is possible for women in hockey, setting a precedent for other sports to follow. The league's impact on women's hockey is multifaceted, encompassing the development of the sport at the grassroots level, providing opportunities for professional growth, and enhancing the visibility and status of women's hockey on the international stage. The NWHL's role in advancing women's hockey has been transformative, paving the way for future generations of female athletes and contributing to the ongoing evolution of the sport.

The Heritage Classic - Hockey's Return to Its Roots

Concept and Planning

The Heritage Classic, a significant event in the National Hockey League (NHL), was conceptualized as a tribute to hockey's origins and its deep-rooted traditions. The idea behind it was to take the professional game back to its outdoor roots, celebrating the sport's history and the natural elements in which it was originally played. This concept resonated with fans and players alike, evoking nostalgia for the days when hockey was played on frozen ponds and outdoor rinks. The inaugural Heritage Classic was held in 2003, and it was the first regular-season NHL game to be played outdoors since the league's inception. The event was inspired in part by the success of the "Cold War" game, a 2001 outdoor collegiate hockey game, which drew significant attention and attendance.

Organizing the Heritage Classic was a monumental task, requiring extensive planning and coordination. The game was set to take place at Commonwealth Stadium in Edmonton, Alberta, a venue traditionally used for Canadian football. Transforming a football stadium into an outdoor hockey arena presented unique logistical challenges. The process involved installing a rink on the football field, ensuring the ice surface remained playable in the fluctuating outdoor conditions, and accommodating the needs of players, officials, and fans in an outdoor setting. The organizers had to consider everything from weather conditions to spectator comfort, making sure that the event was not only a celebration of hockey's heritage but also an enjoyable experience for those in attendance.

The preparation for the Heritage Classic also involved significant efforts to capture the spirit and history of hockey. This included creating a festival-like atmosphere around the game, with various activities and events that celebrated the sport's rich tradition. The planning team worked closely with the participating teams, the Edmonton Oilers and the Montreal Canadiens, two franchises with deep roots in the sport, to ensure that the event paid proper homage to the history and culture of hockey.

The Heritage Classic was not just about the game itself but also about creating a connection between the sport's past and its present, making it a truly special occasion for everyone involved. Its concept and planning showcased the NHL's commitment to honoring the sport's heritage, and the successful execution of the event set the stage for future outdoor games in the league.

The Game Itself

The Heritage Classic game, played between the Montreal Canadiens and the Edmonton Oilers on November 22, 2003, was a remarkable and memorable event in the history of the NHL. The matchup took place in Edmonton's Commonwealth

Stadium, with a massive crowd of over 57,000 fans braving the cold to witness this unique outdoor hockey game. The atmosphere was electric, a blend of excitement and nostalgia, as fans were wrapped in blankets and winter gear, creating a sea of colorful team jerseys and winter hats. The weather was a quintessential element of the game, with temperatures dropping to nearly -18°C (0°F), adding to the authenticity of the outdoor hockey experience.

The game itself was an intriguing battle between two storied franchises. The Montreal Canadiens, one of the NHL's Original Six teams, and the Edmonton Oilers, a team known for its dynasty in the 1980s, provided a compelling storyline for the game. The players, accustomed to the controlled environment of indoor arenas, had to adjust to the outdoor elements, which added a unique challenge to the game. The cold weather affected playing conditions, with the ice being harder and the puck moving differently, requiring players to adapt their style of play.

The Oilers, playing in front of their home crowd, were energized by the atmosphere and the significance of the event. Despite the challenging conditions, both teams showcased their skills, offering a display of top-level hockey that thrilled the fans. The game was a close contest, with both teams demonstrating their resilience and adaptability to the outdoor environment. The Montreal Canadiens ultimately emerged victorious, winning the game 4-3. The outcome, however, was just one aspect of an event that celebrated the spirit and history of hockey

The player experiences during the Heritage Classic were unique and varied. Many players spoke about the surreal feeling of playing in such a large stadium, under the open sky, and in the freezing cold — a stark contrast to the usual indoor rink setting. For some, it was a throwback to their childhood days of playing on outdoor ponds and rinks, bringing back fond memories. The Heritage Classic was more than just a regular season game; it was an experience that left a lasting impression on the players and fans alike. The game's success went beyond the scoreline, as it captured the essence of hockey's roots and its enduring appeal. The Heritage Classic of 2003 was not only a celebration of the sport's history but also a testament to its enduring popularity and the special place it holds in the hearts of players and fans.

Historical Significance

The Heritage Classic held in 2003 was a landmark event in the NHL, marking the league's first regular-season outdoor game. This pioneering event represented a significant moment in the history of professional hockey, acknowledging and celebrating the sport's outdoor origins. Before the advent of indoor ice rinks, hockey was primarily played outdoors, and this event served as a homage to those early days of the sport. The game's setting in the open air, amidst the natural elements, was a nod to the roots of hockey, offering a stark contrast to the modern, indoor version of the game that fans and players had become accustomed to.

The historical significance of the Heritage Classic extended beyond its tribute to the past. It was a groundbreaking moment in the NHL's history, opening up new possibilities for the league in terms of game presentation and fan engagement. The success of the event demonstrated the viability and appeal of outdoor games, leading to the establishment of annual outdoor games in the league's calendar, including the Winter Classic and Stadium Series. These events have since become highly anticipated fixtures, drawing large crowds and offering unique experiences for fans and players alike.

The Heritage Classic also had a broader impact on the sport of hockey, reinforcing its cultural significance and its connection to the natural, winter environment of its origins. The event captured the imagination of fans, evoking a sense of nostalgia and a deeper appreciation for the sport's history and tradition. It showcased hockey in its most elemental form, played under the open sky and in cold temperatures, reminiscent of the conditions under which many players first learned the game.

Furthermore, the Heritage Classic served as a reminder of hockey's ability to adapt and innovate while staying true to its roots. The event was a celebration of the sport's heritage, but it also highlighted the evolution of hockey and its enduring appeal. The historical significance of the Heritage Classic lies in its successful blend of tradition and modernity, creating a memorable experience that honored the past while adding a new chapter to the NHL's history. This event marked a turning point in how the league and its fans celebrate the game, paying tribute to hockey's rich legacy while embracing new ways to enjoy and experience the sport.

Legacy and Future Outdoor Games

The Heritage Classic of 2003 not only celebrated hockey's history but also set a precedent for future outdoor games in the NHL, fundamentally altering the landscape of professional hockey events. Its overwhelming success demonstrated the immense potential and appeal of outdoor hockey games, paving the way for the establishment of annual events like the Winter Classic and the Stadium Series. These events have become marquee fixtures in the NHL calendar, eagerly anticipated by fans and players alike for their unique blend of sport and spectacle.

The Winter Classic, first held in 2008, drew inspiration from the Heritage Classic, taking the concept of outdoor games to new heights. It has been hosted in various iconic stadiums across North America, featuring different teams each year. The Winter Classic is typically held on New Year's Day, becoming a holiday tradition for many hockey fans. It has garnered significant media attention and high viewership, further cementing the popularity of outdoor games. The success of the Winter Classic has demonstrated the enduring appeal of outdoor hockey, showcasing the sport in its elemental form while also providing a unique and entertaining experience.

Similarly, the Stadium Series, introduced in 2014, expanded the concept of outdoor games to more venues and teams. These games are held in large stadiums, often football or baseball stadiums, bringing the excitement of outdoor hockey to new audiences and locations. The Stadium Series has allowed more teams to participate in outdoor games, sharing the experience with a broader range of fans.

Both the Winter Classic and the Stadium Series have become integral parts of the NHL season, offering a distinct and memorable experience that contrasts with the regular indoor games. They have helped to promote the sport to a wider audience, drawing in casual fans and those new to hockey.

The legacy of the Heritage Classic is evident in the continued popularity and expansion of outdoor games in the NHL. These events have become more than just games; they are celebrations of hockey's heritage and a showcase of the sport's ability to evolve while honoring its roots. The success of these outdoor games has also inspired similar events in other hockey leagues and levels, from minor leagues to international competitions, spreading the appeal of outdoor hockey across the globe. The Heritage Classic's influence on the future of outdoor games in the NHL is a clear indication of its significant impact, changing the way hockey is celebrated and experienced by fans and players.

Jarome Iginla's Impact On and Off the Ice

Rising to Stardom with the Flames

Jarome Iginla's journey to becoming a star in the NHL and a key figure for the Calgary Flames is a story of remarkable talent and relentless dedication. Born on July 1, 1977, in Edmonton, Alberta, Canada, Iginla's career in the NHL began when he was drafted by the Dallas Stars in 1995, but he was soon traded to the Calgary Flames, where he would make a profound impact. From his early days with the Flames, Iginla's potential was evident. He possessed a unique combination of skill, physicality, and leadership qualities that quickly set him apart from his peers.

In Calgary, Iginla's progression as a player was rapid and impressive. He became known for his powerful shot, excellent puck-handling skills, and physical style of play. Iginla's ability to consistently score goals, combined with his physical presence on the ice, made him a formidable opponent. He had a natural talent for finding the back of the net and his scoring prowess became a key component of the Flames' offensive strategy. Iginla's leadership skills also came to the forefront early in his career. He was named the captain of the Flames in 2003, a role he would hold for nine seasons. His leadership was not just about his performance on the ice; it also involved his ability to inspire and motivate his teammates, leading by example through his work ethic and dedication to the game.

Iginla's impact on the Flames was transformative. He helped lead the team to several successful seasons, including a memorable run to the Stanley Cup Finals in 2004. During this period, Iginla was at the peak of his career, showcasing his abilities as a top scorer and a leader. He won multiple individual awards, including the Art Ross Trophy as the league's leading scorer and the Lester B. Pearson Award (now known as the Ted Lindsay Award) as the most outstanding player as voted by his peers. These accolades were a testament to his standing as one of the premier players in the league.

Throughout his time with the Flames, Iginla became more than just a star player; he became the face of the franchise. His commitment to the team and the city of Calgary endeared him to the fans, making him a beloved figure in the community. Iginla's rise to stardom with the Flames was not just about his individual achievements; it was also about his ability to elevate the team's performance and create a lasting impact on the franchise. His legacy with the Flames is marked by his incredible contributions on the ice and his role as a leader and an ambassador for the sport.

Key Career Achievements

Jarome Iginla's career is marked by a series of significant achievements that underscore his excellence on the ice and his leadership qualities. One of the most notable aspects of his career was his scoring ability. Iginla achieved several scoring milestones, consistently ranking among the top scorers in the league. He reached the prestigious mark of 50 goals in a season twice, a feat that highlights his prowess as a goal scorer. His ability to find the back of the net with remarkable consistency made him a central figure in the Calgary Flames' offense and a feared opponent for defenses across the NHL.

As the captain of the Calgary Flames, Iginla's leadership was another key aspect of his career achievements. He served as the team's captain from 2003 to 2013, during which he was not only the team's leading scorer but also the heart and soul of the squad. Iginla's leadership extended beyond his on-ice performance; he was known for his ability to inspire and motivate his teammates, setting the tone for the team both in games and in the locker room. His leadership qualities were evident during the Flames' memorable run to the Stanley Cup Finals in 2004, where he played a pivotal role. Iginla's performance in the 2004 playoffs was exceptional, leading the league in scoring during the postseason and almost single-handedly guiding the Flames to the brink of a championship.

Iginla's achievements also include multiple selections to the NHL All-Star Game, reflecting his status as one of the top players in the league. He received the King Clancy Memorial Trophy for his leadership qualities and humanitarian contributions, further demonstrating his impact both on and off the ice. Additionally, he won the Maurice "Rocket" Richard Trophy as the NHL's leading goal scorer and the Art Ross Trophy for leading the league in points, solidifying his reputation as an elite offensive talent.

Throughout his career, Iginla was known for his performance in crucial games. He had a knack for stepping up when the stakes were highest, delivering key goals, and inspiring performances in playoff games and other high-pressure situations. His ability to perform under pressure was a hallmark of his career, making him one of the most reliable and respected players in the league. Iginla's career achievements are a testament to his skill, determination, and leadership, making him one of the most accomplished and revered players of his generation.

Community Involvement and Charity Work

Jarome Iginla's contributions off the ice, particularly his involvement in community and charity work, have been as impactful as his performance on the ice. He has been deeply involved in various community initiatives, demonstrating his commitment to giving back and making a positive difference. One of the key areas of his community involvement has been his support for youth hockey programs. Iginla has been passionate about making hockey accessible to children, especially those who may not have the opportunity to play due to financial barriers. His efforts have included funding and supporting programs that provide equipment and ice time for young players. This commitment to youth hockey has not only helped grow the sport but has also allowed children to experience the joy and benefits of playing hockey.

In addition to his support for youth hockey, Iginla has been involved in a wide range of charitable activities. He has been a major supporter of various causes, including children's health and wellness initiatives. Iginla's charitable work often involves personal interactions with those he is helping, whether it's visiting children in hospitals or participating in community events. He has used his platform as a professional athlete to raise awareness and funds for various charities, showing a genuine passion for helping others.

Iginla's community involvement has also established him as a positive role model, both in Calgary and in the broader hockey community. His approachable and humble nature, combined with his commitment to making a positive impact, has made him an admired figure. Parents, coaches, and players have looked up to him as an example of how professional athletes can use their influence for good. His dedication to community work and charity has been recognized with several awards, further highlighting his contributions off the ice.

Jarome Iginla's legacy in the world of hockey is not limited to his achievements in the NHL but is also defined by his extensive community involvement and charity work. His efforts to support youth hockey, contribute to charitable causes, and serve as a role model have made a lasting impact. Iginla's commitment to giving back and supporting his community has been an integral part of his career, cementing his status as not just a great hockey player, but also a compassionate and dedicated individual.

Legacy in Hockey and Beyond

Jarome Iginla's legacy in hockey and beyond is a remarkable blend of athletic excellence and profound community impact. On the ice, Iginla's career was marked by extraordinary achievements and a playing style that combined skill, physicality, and leadership. He left an indelible mark on the Calgary Flames, becoming the face of the franchise and one of the most respected players in the NHL. His influence within the sport extended beyond his goal-scoring ability and on-ice presence. Iginla was known for his sportsmanship, work ethic, and ability to inspire teammates and fans alike. His impact on hockey was not just about the records he set or the games he won; it was also about the way he played the game and the respect he earned from players, coaches, and hockey enthusiasts.

Off the ice, Iginla's legacy is equally significant, particularly in the Calgary community. His extensive community involvement and charity work have made a lasting impact, demonstrating his commitment to using his platform for the greater good. Through his support for youth hockey programs and various charitable initiatives, Iginla has shown a deep dedication to enriching the lives of others. His efforts have made him a beloved figure in Calgary, revered not just for his athletic achievements but also for his generosity and kindness.

Iginla's influence as a role model cannot be overstated. His career serves as an inspiration to aspiring athletes, showing that success can be achieved with integrity, hard work, and a commitment to excellence. His journey from a young hockey player to an NHL star and community leader embodies the qualities of determination, resilience, and compassion. Iginla's legacy in hockey and beyond is characterized by his impact on the sport, his contributions to his community, and the lasting impression he has left on those who have watched, played with, or been inspired by him. His career is a testament to his exceptional talent and character, making him a true icon in the world of hockey and a cherished member of the Calgary community.

The Evolution of Hockey Safety and Equipment

Early Equipment and Safety Standards

The evolution of hockey safety and equipment has been a journey marked by significant changes and innovations, reflecting the sport's growing concern for player safety. In the early days of hockey, the equipment used by players was rudimentary and provided minimal protection. Early hockey gear was primarily focused on basic functionality, with little consideration given to player safety. Skates were made from leather, with blades attached to the bottom, and pads were hardly more than felt or leather pieces. The protection offered by this early equipment was minimal and players often suffered injuries as a result.

Helmets were not a part of the standard hockey equipment in the initial years. Players often played without any head protection, leading to a high risk of head injuries. The concept of safety gear in hockey evolved slowly, with initial resistance to wearing helmets due to concerns about limited visibility and mobility. It wasn't until the tragic death of Bill Masterton in 1968, who suffered a fatal head injury during an NHL game, that the conversation about mandatory helmet use gained momentum.

Goaltenders, in particular, played a perilous role in the early years of hockey. The original goaltending equipment was barely more than regular pads and lacked any specialized protection for the face. It was common for goaltenders to sustain injuries from pucks hitting their faces. The introduction of the goalie mask, popularized by Jacques Plante in 1959, marked a significant advancement in player safety. Plante's decision to wear a mask in games was initially met with skepticism, but it soon became an essential piece of equipment for goaltenders.

The evolution of hockey equipment in the early years was a gradual process, influenced by a combination of technological advancements and a growing awareness of the importance of player safety. This initial period set the stage for the significant developments in safety gear that would follow, as the hockey community began to prioritize the well-being of its players. The shift towards a safety-conscious approach in hockey equipment marked a critical turning point in the sport, laying the foundation for the comprehensive safety standards and advanced equipment used in modern hockey.

Introduction of Key Safety Gear

The development of safety gear in hockey has seen several key milestones that have significantly enhanced player protection over the years. One of the most crucial advancements was the introduction and eventual mandatory use of helmets. Following Bill Masterton's fatal injury in 1968, the NHL slowly began to recognize the importance of head protection. The transition to widespread helmet use was gradual, with the NHL making helmets mandatory for all new players starting in 1979. This rule change marked a significant shift in attitudes toward player safety, acknowledging the need to protect players from severe head injuries.

Another major milestone in the development of safety gear was the introduction of the goalie mask. Goaltenders, who face the constant threat of high-speed pucks, initially played without any facial protection. The game-changing moment came when Jacques Plante, a goaltender for the Montreal Canadiens, started wearing a mask during games in 1959 after sustaining a facial injury. Plante's mask, initially a simple fiberglass design, set a new standard for goalie equipment, leading to the development of more advanced and protective masks over the years. Today, goalie masks are highly sophisticated, offering superior protection while also becoming a canvas for artistic expression for goaltenders.

Protective padding is another area where significant advancements have been made. Early hockey padding was minimal, often made from felt or leather, and provided limited protection. Over the years, the materials and design of hockey padding have evolved drastically. Modern protective gear, including shoulder pads, elbow pads, shin guards, and gloves, is made from lightweight, impact-absorbing materials. These advancements have greatly reduced the risk of injuries from pucks, sticks, and physical contact.

The introduction of these key pieces of safety gear - helmets, goalie masks, and protective padding - has been instrumental in making hockey a safer sport. These milestones in equipment development reflect a growing commitment to player safety, balancing the physical nature of the sport with measures to protect players from serious injuries. The evolution of safety gear in hockey is a testament to the sport's adaptability and willingness to embrace change for the well-being of its players.

Recent Advances and Protocols

In recent years, the hockey world has seen significant advancements in equipment technology and the implementation of new safety protocols, particularly in the realm of concussion prevention and treatment. These developments are a response to the growing body of research highlighting the serious impact of concussions and other head injuries. One of the most notable advancements is in helmet design and technology. Modern hockey helmets are a far cry from their predecessors, incorporating cutting-edge materials and designs that provide better protection against impacts. These helmets are the result of extensive research and testing, aimed at reducing the force of impacts that can cause concussions. Manufacturers have focused on creating helmets that not only protect the head but also are comfortable and lightweight, encouraging player compliance.

Another significant advancement in hockey safety is the improved understanding and management of concussions. The NHL, along with other hockey organizations, has implemented more rigorous concussion protocols to protect players. These protocols include mandatory assessments for any player who suffers a potential head injury during a game. The shift towards a more cautious approach is evident in the increased duration of rest and recovery required before a player who has suffered a concussion can return to play. This change reflects a growing acknowledgment of the seriousness of concussions and the importance of allowing adequate time for recovery.

In addition to advancements in helmets and concussion protocols, there have been innovations in other protective equipment, such as mouthguards and neck guards. Mouthguards, now designed to absorb more impact, play a crucial role in reducing the risk of concussions. Neck guards, which were once rarely used, have seen increased adoption as they help protect against lacerations and other neck injuries.

Educational initiatives have also been a key part of recent advances in hockey safety. These programs aim to inform players, coaches, and parents about the risks associated with concussions and the importance of proper equipment use. Education is critical in fostering a culture of safety in the sport, ensuring that all stakeholders are aware of the best practices for preventing and managing injuries.

Overall, the recent advances in equipment technology and safety protocols in hockey represent a significant step forward in the sport's ongoing effort to protect its players. By focusing on concussion prevention and treatment, and continually improving protective equipment, hockey is evolving to meet the challenges posed by a fast-paced, physical sport. These developments are essential in ensuring that players can compete safely and at their best, now and in the future.

Impact on the Game

The advancements in hockey safety and equipment have had a profound impact on how the game is played, bringing about a shift in both player behavior and the overall approach to the sport. The increased focus on safety, particularly concerning head injuries, has influenced the rules and playing style in hockey. There has been a noticeable move towards penalizing and reducing dangerous plays, such as hits to the head and boarding, which pose high risks for concussions and other serious injuries. This shift has prompted players to adapt their style of play, becoming more mindful of safety while still maintaining the physical intensity that is a hallmark of hockey.

The improvements in protective gear, including more advanced helmets and padding, have also allowed players to engage in the sport with a greater sense of security. Knowing that they are better protected, players can focus more on their performance and skills, potentially leading to a faster, more skill-oriented style of play. The evolution of equipment has not only enhanced safety but has also contributed to the development of the game, with players able to execute plays and maneuvers that might have been riskier with older, less effective gear.

Moreover, the ongoing efforts to balance player safety with the physical nature of hockey have led to a greater emphasis on player education and health awareness. Players are now more informed about the risks associated with the sport, including the long-term impacts of injuries like concussions. This awareness has fostered a culture of safety in hockey, where players are encouraged to take precautions, properly use safety equipment, and report injuries when they occur.

These changes have extended beyond the professional leagues, impacting youth and amateur hockey as well. The emphasis on safety and proper equipment use at younger ages is shaping a new generation of players who are more conscious of the importance of safety in hockey. This evolution in the approach to safety is seen as crucial for the long-term health and well-being of players and for the sustainability of the sport itself.

The impact of these safety and equipment advancements on the game of hockey is significant. While preserving the sport's inherent physicality and excitement, these changes are ensuring that hockey can be played in a safer, more responsible manner. The ongoing efforts to balance safety with the physical nature of the sport are fundamental in adapting hockey to contemporary understandings of athlete health and safety, ultimately benefiting players at all levels of the game.

Bobby Orr's Revolutionary Play as a Defenseman

Early Career and Entry into the NHL

Bobby Orr's journey to becoming one of the most revolutionary players in hockey history began long before he made his mark with the Boston Bruins. Born on March 20, 1948, in Parry Sound, Ontario, Orr displayed an extraordinary talent for hockey from a young age. Growing up in a small town, Orr honed his skills on local rinks, quickly standing out for his exceptional skating ability and understanding of the game. His early years were characterized by a deep passion for hockey and a work ethic that set him apart from his peers. Orr's talent was evident, and he soon caught the attention of scouts across Canada.

As a teenager, Orr's career took a significant turn when he joined the Oshawa Generals, a junior team in the Ontario Hockey Association. It was here that Orr began to develop the skills and style of play that would later define his career in the NHL. Even at this early stage, Orr's play was revolutionary. As a defenseman, he was not content to limit his role to traditional defensive duties; instead, he actively involved himself in offensive plays, showcasing his remarkable skating and puck-handling skills. This approach to the defenseman position was unconventional at the time, but Orr's success with it was undeniable.

Orr's entry into the NHL came in 1966 when he signed with the Boston Bruins. His debut was highly anticipated, and he did not disappoint. From his first season, Orr's impact on the team was transformative. He brought a new dynamism to the Bruins' defense, contributing significantly to both offensive and defensive plays. His ability to control the game, combined with his speed and agility, made him a standout player from the outset. Orr's innovative style of play began to challenge the traditional perceptions of the role of a defenseman in hockey.

Orr's early years with the Bruins were marked by individual achievements and a clear indication of his potential to change the game. He won the Calder Trophy as the league's best rookie, a sign of the significant impact he was already having in the NHL. Orr's presence on the ice was electrifying, and he quickly became one of the most exciting players to watch. His entry into the NHL and initial years with the Bruins set the stage for what would become a legendary career, marked by unparalleled achievements and a revolutionary approach to the defenseman position. Bobby Orr's early career and entry into the NHL were the beginnings of a journey that would see him redefine the role of a defenseman and leave a lasting legacy in the world of hockey.

Transforming the Defenseman Role

Bobby Orr's transformation of the defenseman role in hockey was nothing short of revolutionary. Prior to Orr's arrival in the

NHL, defensemen were primarily expected to focus on preventing scoring opportunities, with limited involvement in offensive plays. Orr, however, redefined this position with his unique playstyle, blending defensive responsibilities with a strong offensive presence. His approach to the game was characterized by an unparalleled skating ability. Orr's speed and agility on the ice allowed him to move effortlessly between defense and offense, breaking away from traditional defensive roles. His skating wasn't just about speed; it was about control and the ability to maneuver through opponents with ease. This mobility enabled him to support his team's offensive plays while still fulfilling his defensive duties.

Orr's offensive playstyle as a defenseman was groundbreaking. He was not content to simply pass the puck to forwards; instead, he actively participated in creating scoring opportunities. Orr had an exceptional ability to read the game, anticipating plays and making decisive moves that often led to goals or goal opportunities. His skill in handling the puck, combined with his speed, made him a formidable force on the offensive front. He had the rare ability to lead an attack, weaving through opposing players and setting up plays or scoring himself. This offensive contribution from a defenseman was innovative and changed the way the position was played.

Orr's game intelligence was another key factor in his transformation of the defenseman role. He had a deep understanding of the game, allowing him to make smart decisions quickly. Orr could assess situations on the ice with remarkable clarity, knowing when to push forward into an offensive play and when to hang back and focus on defense. His vision of the game was holistic; he understood the importance of positioning, timing, and strategy, both for himself and his team.

Bobby Orr's impact on the defenseman role had a lasting effect on the sport of hockey. He showed that defensemen could be integral to a team's offense without compromising their defensive responsibilities. His style inspired future generations of defensemen to adopt a more dynamic and involved approach to the position. Orr's legacy in transforming the defenseman role is reflected in the way the position is played today, with many defensemen now actively contributing to their team's offensive play, a shift that can be attributed largely to Orr's revolutionary approach to the game.

Career Highlights and Achievements

Bobby Orr's career is adorned with a multitude of highlights and achievements that underscore his status as one of the greatest hockey players of all time. Throughout his career, Orr accumulated an impressive array of awards and records, setting new standards for excellence in the sport. One of Orr's most significant achievements was his collection of Norris Trophies. Awarded annually to the NHL's top defenseman, the Norris Trophy became almost synonymous with Orr during his career. He won the award an unprecedented eight consecutive times from 1968 to 1975, a testament to his dominance in the defenseman role and his all-around excellence on the ice.

In addition to his individual accolades, Orr's contributions to team success were equally remarkable. He was instrumental in leading the Boston Bruins to Stanley Cup victories in 1970 and 1972. Orr's performance in the 1970 Stanley Cup playoffs was particularly memorable, culminating in the iconic overtime goal that clinched the championship for the Bruins. This moment, captured in a famous photograph of Orr flying through the air after scoring, has become one of the most enduring images in hockey history. Orr's impact in the Stanley Cup victories went beyond scoring; he was a key player in all aspects of the game, from defense to creating scoring opportunities.

Orr's record-setting performances extended to various aspects of the game. He was the first defenseman in NHL history to score over 100 points in a season, a feat he achieved three times in his career. His offensive production from the defenseman position was unprecedented, redefining what was considered possible for players in that role. Orr also set the record for most points in a single season by a defenseman, a record that stood for decades. His ability to consistently score and assist while fulfilling defensive responsibilities was unmatched.

Orr's career was not just about the accumulation of awards and records; it was about the way he played the game. His dynamic and skillful style of play brought a new level of excitement to hockey, captivating fans and inspiring future generations of players. Orr's achievements on the ice have left a lasting legacy, securing his place in the annals of hockey history as one of the sport's most exceptional and influential players. His career highlights and achievements are a reflection of his unique talent, his dedication to the sport, and his impact on the game of hockey.

Legacy in Hockey

Bobby Orr's lasting impact on the sport of hockey is immeasurable, transcending his impressive list of achievements and records. Orr revolutionized the role of the defenseman, transforming it from a primarily defensive position into one that is integral to the offensive dynamics of the game. His style of play, characterized by exceptional skating, offensive prowess, and defensive skill, redefined what it meant to be a defenseman. Orr's influence on the sport can be seen in the generations of defensemen who followed him. Many have emulated his style, blending defensive responsibilities with offensive contributions, a testament to Orr's lasting impact on the position. His legacy is evident in the way defensemen are evaluated and utilized in the modern game, with greater emphasis on versatility and offensive ability.

Beyond his technical contributions to the sport, Orr's impact on hockey is also reflected in the way he inspired future generations of players. His exciting, dynamic style of play captivated fans and aspiring hockey players alike, making him a role model for many who took up the sport. Orr's passion for hockey, coupled with his humility and sportsmanship, endeared him to fans and players, making his influence on the sport more than just his on-ice accomplishments. Orr's approach to the game, marked by innovation and excellence, has left a lasting mark on hockey, inspiring players to push the boundaries of their positions and abilities.

Recognized as one of the greatest players in NHL history, Orr's legacy is not confined to the records he set or the trophies he won. It is also about the lasting changes he brought to the game. His impact on hockey is seen in the way the sport has evolved since his playing days, with defensemen now playing a more prominent role in the offensive play of their teams. Orr's legacy in hockey is a blend of his groundbreaking contributions to the sport, his inspirational influence on players and fans, and his status as a hockey icon. His name is synonymous with excellence in hockey, and his legacy continues to be celebrated by those who appreciate the profound impact he had on the sport.

The Expansion of Hockey Globally

Growth in Non-Traditional Markets

The expansion of hockey globally has seen the sport's footprint extend into countries and regions not traditionally associated with ice hockey. This growth reflects the sport's increasing appeal and the efforts to promote hockey beyond its customary strongholds in North America and Europe. Countries like Australia, China, and various nations in the Middle East have witnessed a notable rise in interest and participation in hockey, signaling a shift in the sport's geographic reach.

In Australia, a country more known for its warm climate and love for sports like cricket and rugby, hockey has been steadily gaining ground. The Australian Ice Hockey League (AIHL), established in 2000, has played a significant role in this growth. The league, though semi-professional, has attracted local talent and a few international players, helping to raise the profile of the sport. Ice rinks, once a rarity in Australia, have become more prevalent, providing opportunities for people to learn and play hockey. Australian players are increasingly making their mark, with some even pursuing opportunities in North American and European leagues.

China's engagement with hockey has been part of a broader push to develop winter sports, especially ahead of hosting the 2022 Winter Olympics in Beijing. The Chinese government has invested in building ice rinks and developing hockey programs at the grassroots level. The inclusion of a Chinese team, the Kunlun Red Star, in the Kontinental Hockey League (KHL), has been a significant step in raising the sport's profile in the country. These efforts are aimed not only at fostering local talent but also at building a fan base for hockey in a nation where it has historically been a minor sport.

In the Middle East, countries like the United Arab Emirates (UAE) and Qatar have seen a surprising growth in hockey's popularity. In the UAE, the Emirates Hockey League, formed in 2009, has brought together players of various nationalities residing in the country. The availability of ice rinks in malls and recreational centers in the region has made the sport more accessible to the public. These countries have also hosted international hockey events, further contributing to the sport's growth and visibility in the region.

The expansion of hockey into non-traditional markets is a significant development for the sport, indicating its growing global appeal. This growth is not just about the professional or elite level of play; it's also about grassroots development and the introduction of the sport to new audiences. The spread of hockey into countries with no historical connection to the sport suggests a changing landscape, where the appeal of hockey transcends traditional geographical and climatic boundaries.

This expansion is a positive sign for the sport, promising a more diverse and global hockey community in the future.

International Players in the NHL

The National Hockey League (NHL) has seen a significant increase in the number of international players, a trend that has enriched the league and broken down national stereotypes in the sport. Players from a diverse range of countries have not only found their way into the NHL but have also made substantial impacts with their teams. This influx of international talent has brought new styles of play, different perspectives, and a global flavor to the league, enhancing the overall competitiveness and appeal of the NHL.

Traditionally dominated by Canadian and American players, the NHL's landscape began to change as more players from European countries, such as Sweden, Finland, Russia, and the Czech Republic, entered the league. These players brought with them a unique set of skills and approaches to the game, influenced by their home countries' playing styles. European players are often known for their strong skating abilities, technical skills, and strategic understanding of the game. Their presence in the NHL has introduced new tactics and techniques, contributing to the evolution of hockey in North America.

In recent years, the NHL has seen a growing number of players from countries not traditionally known for ice hockey. Nations like Switzerland, Germany, and Slovakia, among others, have produced NHL players who have defied stereotypes and excelled at the highest level of the sport. These players have overcome the challenges of developing their skills in countries with fewer resources and opportunities for hockey, demonstrating that talent and dedication can emerge from any corner of the globe.

The impact of international players in the NHL extends beyond their on-ice performance. They serve as role models and sources of inspiration in their home countries, encouraging the growth of hockey and the development of future talents. The success of these players in the NHL has helped to promote the sport globally, showing aspiring hockey players around the world that reaching the NHL is an achievable goal regardless of their nationality.

The increasing diversity of players in the NHL is a positive development for the league, fostering a more inclusive and global hockey community. It challenges the notion that hockey is a sport limited to certain countries, showcasing the universal appeal and reach of the game. The contributions of international players have not only enhanced the level of competition in the NHL but have also played a crucial role in expanding the sport's fan base and visibility across the world.

Global Tournaments and International Success

International tournaments, notably the Olympics and the Ice Hockey World Championships, have played a pivotal role in popularizing hockey on a global scale. These events showcase the sport at its highest level, bringing together the world's best players to compete on an international stage. The impact of these tournaments extends far beyond the ice, as they captivate audiences worldwide and introduce hockey to new fans.

The Olympics, in particular, have been a significant platform for the growth of hockey. The inclusion of ice hockey in the Winter Olympics has provided the sport with tremendous exposure and prestige. Hockey games at the Olympics consistently draw large viewerships, partly due to the tournament's format that brings national pride into play. The fierce competition between countries creates riveting narratives and unforgettable moments that resonate with viewers. Olympic hockey has seen some historic moments, such as the "Miracle on Ice" in 1980, which not only had a profound impact in the United States but also captured the imagination of sports fans around the world.

The Ice Hockey World Championships, organized by the International Ice Hockey Federation (IIHF), is another significant event in the hockey calendar. The tournament offers a unique blend of established hockey nations and emerging teams, providing a platform for lesser-known hockey countries to compete against traditional powerhouses. This exposure is invaluable for the development of the sport in these countries, offering their players experience against top-level competition and their fans a chance to see world-class hockey.

These international tournaments also play a key role in showcasing the diversity and global nature of the sport. Players from various national leagues come together to represent their countries, demonstrating the widespread talent and reach of hockey. The success of nations like Finland, Sweden, Canada, and Russia in these tournaments highlights the depth and quality of hockey talent worldwide.

Moreover, the international tournaments serve as catalysts for the development of hockey programs in participating countries. Success or strong performances in these tournaments often lead to increased interest and investment in the sport at the grassroots level. They inspire a new generation of players and fans, contributing to the growth of hockey in both traditional and non-traditional markets.

The global tournaments' role in popularizing hockey is evident in the increasing parity seen in international competition. The gap between hockey's traditional powerhouses and emerging nations has been narrowing, indicating the sport's growth and development worldwide. These tournaments not only provide entertainment and showcase high-level hockey but also contribute significantly to spreading the sport's popularity across the globe, making hockey a truly international game.

Development Programs and Grassroots Growth

The growth of hockey at the grassroots level in various regions across the globe is largely attributed to the concerted efforts of organizations like the National Hockey League (NHL), the International Ice Hockey Federation (IIHF), and other hockey bodies. These organizations have implemented a range of development programs and initiatives aimed at fostering the growth of hockey from the ground up. These efforts are pivotal in introducing the sport to new audiences and nurturing the next generation of hockey talent.

The NHL has been proactive in promoting hockey's growth beyond its traditional markets, realizing the potential for expanding its global fan base. The league has undertaken various initiatives, including hosting games and events in non-traditional hockey countries, to expose more people to the sport. The NHL's outreach efforts often involve community-based programs that introduce hockey to children in a fun and engaging manner. These programs typically provide access to equipment and training, making the sport more accessible to youngsters who might not otherwise have the opportunity to play hockey.

The IIHF has played a fundamental role in developing hockey worldwide, particularly in countries where the sport is still emerging. Through its development programs, the IIHF provides resources, coaching, and training to help establish and improve hockey programs. These initiatives are often aimed at developing the sport at all levels, from youth to professional, and include both player development and the training of coaches and officials. The IIHF's efforts are vital in laying a strong foundation for the sport's growth in these new regions.

Besides the NHL and IIHF, various other organizations and hockey federations across the world are involved in grassroots hockey development. These bodies work at the local level to promote the sport, organize leagues and tournaments, and provide young players with avenues to play and develop their skills. The collaboration between local and international bodies is essential for ensuring the sustainable growth of hockey in these regions.

These development programs are not just about growing the sport's popularity; they are also focused on fostering inclusive and diverse growth. Efforts are made to encourage participation from all demographics, including initiatives to increase the involvement of women and underrepresented communities in hockey.

The impact of these development programs and grassroots initiatives is profound. They are creating new opportunities for people to engage with hockey, whether as players, coaches, fans, or officials. By investing in the grassroots growth of hockey, the NHL, IIHF, and other organizations are building a strong, diverse, and global hockey community, ensuring the sport's vitality and relevance for years to come.

References

Adkisson, Dan. *Which Countries Have the Fastest Expanding Hockey Leagues?* Mayor's Manor (2021). https://mayorsmanor.com/2021/10/which-countries-have-the-fastest-expanding-hockey-leagues/. Accessed December 05, 2023.

Enright, Greg. *The Pittsburgh Penguins: The First 25 Years.* McFarland, Incorporated, Publishers (2020)

Falcon, Laura. *1980 Miracle on Ice: Greatest Moment in Sports History Will Never Get Old.* Bleacher Report (2011). https://bleacherreport.com/articles/568574-1980-miracle-on-ice-greatest-moment-in-sports-history-will-never-get-old. Accessed December 01, 2023.

Orr, Bobby. *Orr: My Story.* Penguin Canada (2013).

Payne, C. F. *Breaking the Ice: The True Story of the First Woman to Play in the National Hockey League.* Simon & Schuster/Paula Wiseman Books (2020).

Salvian, Hailey. *Jarome Iginla's Hall of Fame career, in 20 stories not often told: 'Everything he does, he wants to beat you'.* The Athletic (2021). https://theathletic.com/2955394/2021/11/15/jarome-iginlas-hall-of-fame-career-in-20-stories-not-often-told-everything-he-does-he-wants-to-beat-you/. Accessed November 29, 2023

Sollid, Matt. *How hockey gear has changed over the years.* The Rink Live (2022). https://www.therinklive.com/inside-trl/how-hockey-gear-has-changed-over-the-years. Accessed December 04, 2023

The Canadian Encyclopedia. *Wayne Gretzky.* The Canadian Encyclopedia (2009). https://www.thecanadianencyclopedia.ca/en/article/wayne-gretzky. Accessed December 02, 2023

Bonus: Free Book!

Are you ready to delve into the thrilling book in the series, absolutely free? Get ready to go deep into the world of yet another football legend! Just use your smartphone or tablet to scan the QR code below, then follow the simple prompts to receive the PDF.

www.ingramcontent.com/pod-product-compliance
Lightning Source LLC
Chambersburg PA
CBHW052104110526
44591CB00013B/2345